JOSH STEVE

The American Nightmare

Contents

The Calm Before the Storm

The early morning sun cast a warm glow over the small town of Millington as the citizens woke to what seemed like any other day. The smell of fresh coffee wafted through the air as people bustled about, their routines unfolding with a sense of normalcy. Yet, beneath the surface, an undercurrent of tension simmered, and the promise of change hung heavy in the air.

John Mitchell, a middle-aged history teacher with a salt-and-pepper beard, strolled into the local diner, the familiar jingle of the bell announcing his arrival. The place buzzed with chatter as locals sipped coffee and discussed the upcoming election. John couldn't help but notice the palpable excitement mixed with nervous energy.

The 2024 election had become more than just a political event; it was a referendum on the nation's identity, a crossroads where the path to the future lay uncertain. John ordered his usual black coffee and took a seat by the window, watching as families walked by, their children clutching miniature American flags.

As he sipped his coffee, John's mind wandered back to his history classes. He had often taught his students about the resilience of the American democratic experiment, emphasizing the importance of civic duty and the power of the people's voice. Yet, in the current climate, that very foundation seemed to be trembling.

Outside the diner, campaign posters adorned every available surface, each one a declaration of the competing visions for the nation's future. The incumbent president, a seasoned politician with a calming demeanor, promised stability and unity. The challenger, a charismatic outsider, vowed to shake up the establishment and return power to the people.

John couldn't escape the feeling that this election was different. The usual political debates had escalated into bitter arguments among friends and family. The airwaves were saturated with accusations of corruption and conspiracy, leaving the public on edge.

Leaving the diner, John walked through the town square, observing the hustle and bustle of election day. The local polling station, usually a quiet hub of democracy, now buzzed with activity. Lines stretched down the block as citizens waited patiently to cast their votes, their faces reflecting a mix of determination and uncertainty.

At the polling booth, John carefully marked his choices, his hand hesitating for a moment over the ballot. The weight of responsibility hung heavy on him as he considered the implications of his vote. The future of the nation seemed to rest on the shoulders of each individual in that room.

Exiting the polling station, John encountered Sarah Turner, a fellow teacher and longtime friend. Her eyes betrayed a mixture of excitement and anxiety as they locked onto each other.

"John, can you believe it's come to this?" she sighed, her voice tinged with worry.

He nodded, a somber expression on his face. "It feels like we're at a crossroads, Sarah. No matter the outcome, things won't be the same."

As they walked together, the conversation turned to the broader issues facing the nation. The economy, healthcare, foreign relations—the topics that once sparked intellectual debates now carried an urgency that left little room for detached discussion.

By afternoon, social media was ablaze with discussions, arguments, and the occasional plea for unity. The digital realm, once a platform for connecting people, had become a battleground where words were the weapons and friendships the casualties.

That evening, as the polls closed and the nation held its collective breath, John gathered with friends at a local bar to watch the election results unfold on the big screen. The atmosphere was tense, the air thick with anticipation.

As the first states were called, the room erupted into cheers and groans, each reaction a reflection of the political leanings of those present. The noise level rose with each passing moment, and John found himself caught in the emotional whirlwind of the crowd.

As the night wore on, it became clear that the election would not be a swift and decisive victory for either candidate. Battleground states remained undecided, and allegations of irregularities began to surface. The initial excitement transformed into a sense of unease, a realization that the journey ahead might be far bumpier than anyone had anticipated.

The bar emptied out, the patrons dispersing into the night with heavy hearts. John walked home alone, the echoes of the day's events reverberating in his mind. The calm before the storm had passed, and the nation held its breath, unaware of the turbulent path that lay ahead.

In the solitude of his living room, John turned on the television, watching as pundits dissected the election results. The talking heads, normally composed and analytical, now spoke with a sense of urgency. The nation, once again, stood on the precipice of history, and no one could predict what the dawn would bring.

As he turned off the television, John couldn't shake the feeling that the calm before the storm had been replaced by an unsettling stillness, a silence that foreshadowed the turbulence yet to come. The 2024 election had set in motion a series of events that would challenge the very fabric of American democracy, and John Mitchell, like millions of others, braced himself for the storm that loomed on the horizon.

Election Day

The sun rose on Election Day, casting a golden glow over Millington. The town's streets were adorned with campaign signs, each one a testament to the democratic process that had defined the nation for centuries. For Lucy Rodriguez, a small-business owner and lifelong resident of Millington, this day held a mix of excitement and trepidation.

Lucy owned a quaint bookstore on Main Street, a place that had been a community hub for generations. As she unlocked the shop, she couldn't escape the feeling that the air itself was charged with a unique energy. She glanced at the clock, knowing that the town's polling station would soon open its doors.

As Lucy arranged the new arrivals on the shelves, she overheard snippets of conversation from customers discussing the election. The diversity of opinions within the small town was evident, and Lucy marveled at how the same community could hold such a spectrum of beliefs.

The bell above the door chimed, announcing the arrival of Emma Thompson, a high school student who often sought refuge in the bookstore. Emma's eyes sparkled with a mixture of excitement and anxiety.

"Hey, Lucy," Emma greeted. "Did you vote yet?"

Lucy smiled, appreciating the eagerness of the younger generation to participate in the democratic process. "Not yet, Emma. I'm planning to head over soon. Are you old enough to vote?"

Emma nodded, a sense of pride in her voice. "First time voter right here. It feels like the whole town is buzzing about it."

As Lucy engaged in conversation with Emma, she couldn't help but reflect on the historical significance of the day. The right to vote was a cornerstone of American identity, a privilege that generations had fought to secure. Yet, in the current climate, that privilege seemed both sacred and precarious.

The clock on the wall seemed to tick louder as Lucy closed the bookstore for a brief break. She walked towards the polling station, the line of voters extending around the block. A sense of unity permeated the air as people from all walks of life waited patiently, their shared purpose transcending the differences that often divided them.

Lucy joined the line, her mind wandering to the choices she would make on the ballot. The weight of responsibility settled on her shoulders as she considered the candidates and the visions they represented. The future of the nation rested in those choices, and Lucy felt a solemn determination to make her voice heard.

As she approached the entrance of the polling station, Lucy was struck by the diversity of the crowd. Elderly couples with weathered faces, young parents juggling children, and solitary individuals lost in thought—all stood together in the shared act of casting their votes.

Inside the station, the hum of democracy in action resonated. Volunteers checked voter registrations, and the rhythmic sound of ballots being cast filled the room. Lucy approached her designated booth, the curtain closing behind her as she took a moment to absorb the gravity of the moment.

The choices before her were more than names on a ballot; they represented competing visions for the nation's future. Lucy carefully marked her selections, a mixture of hope and uncertainty coursing through her veins. As she exited the booth, she placed her ballot in the box, the sound of it sliding in echoing the culmination of her civic duty.

Outside, Lucy encountered her neighbor, Mr. Johnson, a retired war veteran with a steadfast commitment to the democratic process. His presence exuded a sense of wisdom and resilience, a living testament to the sacrifices made to protect the freedoms that Election Day celebrated.

"Lucy," Mr. Johnson greeted with a warm smile, "voting done?"

Lucy nodded, a sense of camaraderie forming between them. "Yes, Mr. Johnson. It's always a special feeling, isn't it?"

He chuckled, a twinkle in his eyes. "Been doing it for decades, and it never loses its significance. It's a reminder that we're part of something bigger than ourselves."

As they walked back to the town square together, Lucy couldn't help but be moved by the shared experience of Election Day. The town's residents, despite their differences, had come together to exercise a right that defined the very essence of their nation.

The day unfolded with a sense of ceremony as the sun reached its zenith. A local band played patriotic tunes in the square, and food vendors lined the streets, creating an atmosphere that blended festivity with solemnity. Families gathered, children waved flags, and the community, for a brief moment, set aside its divisions.

In the late afternoon, Lucy returned to her bookstore, the events of the day etched into her memory. The news on the radio buzzed with updates on voter turnout and early projections. The anticipation that had simmered for weeks now reached a fever pitch.

As evening descended, Lucy closed the bookstore early, eager to join the community at the local bar, a gathering place for townsfolk to watch the election results unfold. The atmosphere there was charged with tension and excitement as the large television screen broadcasted the first glimpses of the unfolding drama.

Friends and neighbors filled the bar, their eyes glued to the screen. The initial results flashed across, and a murmur of anticipation swept through the room. Lucy found herself standing beside Emma, the two of them sharing a quiet moment of reflection.

The room erupted into cheers and applause as certain states were called. The atmosphere was electric, the highs and lows of the election playing out in real-time. Lucy couldn't escape the emotional rollercoaster, feeling the weight of the nation's collective hopes and fears.

However, as the night wore on, the initial jubilation gave way to a growing sense of uncertainty. Battleground states remained too close to call, and the anchors on the television struggled to make sense of the unfolding narrative. The mood in the bar shifted from celebration to a more somber contemplation of what lay ahead.

Lucy glanced around, seeing the faces of her fellow townspeople etched with concern. The election, which was meant to be a celebration of democracy, now felt like a test of the nation's resilience. The divisions that had simmered beneath the surface were laid bare, and the outcome held the potential to either heal or exacerbate those wounds.

As the clock neared midnight, the bar's patrons began to disperse, their initial excitement tempered by the growing realization that the election results might not be known for days. Lucy walked home in the quiet night, the streets empty and the air heavy with anticipation.

Arriving at her doorstep, Lucy gazed at the stars overhead, a sense of introspection settling upon her. The events of Election Day had been a testament to the strength and fragility of democracy. The choices made by individuals, like ripples in a pond, had far-reaching consequences that would shape the nation's destiny.

Lucy entered her home, the soft glow of her porch light casting a warm welcome. She turned on the television, watching the anchors dissect the results and analyze the path forward. The familiar faces on the screen seemed as uncertain as the rest of the nation, their predictions and analyses unable to provide the clarity that the people sought.

As Lucy prepared for bed, she couldn't escape the feeling that the calm before the storm had given way to a new kind of uncertainty. Election Day, meant to be a celebration of democracy, had become a prologue to a story that would test the resilience of the American spirit.

The town slept in restless anticipation, the outcome of the 2024 election hanging like a question mark over the nation's collective

consciousness. Lucy lay in bed, her thoughts a whirlwind of hopes, fears, and the shared experience of a day that would be etched into the annals of history.

In the darkness, as the clock ticked towards a new day, Lucy closed her eyes, knowing that the dawn would bring not only a new morning but a new chapter in the unfolding saga of the American nightmare.

The Allegations

The morning after Election Day dawned with an air of uncertainty. Millington awoke to a town divided, the optimism of the previous day replaced by whispers of doubt and suspicion. Lucy Rodriguez, like many others, found herself drawn to the news, eager to understand the unfolding narrative that would shape the nation's future.

The local diner, usually abuzz with chatter and the clinking of cutlery, felt somber. As Lucy entered, she noticed the hushed conversations and furrowed brows that reflected the collective mood. The television mounted on the wall broadcasted news anchors discussing allegations of irregularities in the election process.

Taking her usual seat by the window, Lucy ordered a cup of coffee, the warmth of the ceramic mug offering a small comfort in the face of the growing unease. The headlines in the newspapers scattered across the diner painted a picture of a nation grappling with the aftermath of a closely contested election.

John Mitchell, the history teacher, entered the diner, his face a mirror of the town's collective concern. He approached Lucy, a sense of camaraderie born out of shared experience.

"Lucy," he greeted, "have you been following the news?"

She nodded, her eyes reflecting a mixture of weariness and concern. "It's like the unity of Election Day has given way to something else. What's happening to our democracy?"

John sighed, his gaze fixed on the television screen. "These allegations, Lucy, they're tearing at the very fabric of our system. It's unprecedented."

As the two friends delved into conversation, the door swung open, and Emma Thompson rushed in, her eyes wide with a mix of excitement and disbelief.

"Did you see this?" Emma exclaimed, brandishing her smartphone. "There are reports of fraud and manipulation all over social media. It's chaos out there!"

The news had spread like wildfire, and the diner's patrons exchanged glances, the gravity of the situation sinking in. The allegations were not confined to a single state; they sprawled across the nation, casting a shadow over the integrity of the electoral process.

Outside, the town square, which had been a scene of celebration just days before, now bore witness to a gathering storm. Protesters, with signs bearing slogans of both support and dissent, gathered in clusters. Tensions simmered beneath the surface, and the unity that once defined the community now seemed fragile.

Lucy, John, and Emma left the diner, joining the flow of people moving toward the heart of the town. The air crackled with a charged energy, and as they reached the square, the trio observed the unfolding scenes of dissent.

A podium had been erected, and a figure, passionate and articulate, addressed the growing crowd. It was Michael Donovan, a charismatic local leader who had quickly risen to prominence in the wake of the election. His words resonated with the frustrations of those who felt their voices had been muffled.

"The people deserve the truth!" Michael declared, his voice cutting through the tense air. "We won't stand idly by as our democracy is undermined. We demand transparency!"

The crowd responded with a mix of cheers and applause, the discontented murmurs of the people transforming into a chorus of collective frustration. Lucy couldn't help but feel a sense of déjà vu, as if the pages of history were repeating themselves in a dissonant symphony.

As the day unfolded, Millington became a microcosm of the national turmoil. The allegations of fraud were not confined to one side; both the incumbent president and the challenger pointed fingers at each other. The news outlets, once seen as pillars of truth, became battlegrounds of conflicting narratives.

Lucy, John, and Emma found themselves caught in the maelstrom of information and disinformation. Social media, a platform meant to connect people, now fueled the flames of discord. Friends became adversaries in the digital realm, each post and comment a battleground in the ideological war that raged online.

The diner, once a haven of community, now hosted heated debates among its patrons. Lucy observed as friendships strained under the weight of differing beliefs. The very act of civil discourse, once a hallmark of democracy, seemed to be slipping away.

In the midst of the chaos, Lucy's bookstore became a refuge for those seeking solace and a respite from the relentless onslaught of information. The familiar scent of books and the hushed ambiance offered a temporary escape from the cacophony outside.

One afternoon, as Lucy organized a shelf of new arrivals, a familiar face entered the store. It was Mr. Johnson, the war veteran, his expression a blend of weariness and determination.

"Lucy," he greeted, his eyes conveying a depth of experience, "this reminds me of times I thought were long behind us. The nation is tearing itself apart."

She nodded, grateful for the presence of someone who had weathered storms in the past. "It feels like we're on the precipice of something, Mr. Johnson. The unity we felt on Election Day—it's slipping away."

He sighed, running a hand through his silver hair. "It's easy to forget that democracy is a fragile thing. It requires constant vigilance and a commitment to the principles that bind us together. Once those bonds start to fray, it's a slippery slope."

The days turned into weeks, and the allegations continued to cast a dark shadow over the nation. Legal challenges were mounted, and courtrooms became arenas where the fate of democracy hung in the balance. Lucy, John, and Emma attended town hall meetings, where impassioned citizens voiced their concerns and grievances.

In the town square, the protests continued to swell, the air thick with a sense of urgency. Michael Donovan, the charismatic leader, emerged as a prominent voice of dissent. He articulated the frustrations of those who felt marginalized by the political establishment, channeling the collective anger into a call for accountability.

One evening, Lucy found herself drawn to the town square, where Michael Donovan addressed a sea of people, his voice a rallying cry for change. The setting sun cast long shadows on the faces of the protesters, their silhouettes a testament to the depth of their conviction.

"We won't be silenced!" Michael proclaimed, his words echoing off the buildings. "This is our democracy, and we demand answers. We demand justice!"

As the crowd roared in agreement, Lucy felt a knot tighten in her stomach. The divisions that had once seemed like distant thunder now rumbled overhead. The American nightmare, born out of allegations and uncertainty, was consuming the very essence of the nation.

The weeks turned into a month, and the situation showed no signs of resolution. The legal battles continued, each court ruling met with fervent reactions from both sides. Lucy's bookstore became a gathering place for those seeking information, a haven for reasoned discourse in the midst of a cacophony of discord.

One afternoon, Emma entered the bookstore, her eyes reflecting a weariness beyond her years. The weight of the situation pressed upon her shoulders, and she collapsed into a chair.

"Lucy," she sighed, "it feels like we're in a never-ending nightmare. How did it come to this?"

Lucy, too, felt the fatigue of uncertainty, the relentless barrage of information taking its toll. "Emma, in times like these, it's important to remember that change often arises from the darkest moments. We have to hold onto hope and the belief that the collective will of the people can guide us through."

The days stretched into a blur of tension and

unrest. Millington, once a haven of tranquility, now echoed with the sounds of passionate discourse and the occasional clash of opposing ideologies. The town had become a microcosm of the nation, grappling with the consequences of a democracy teetering on the edge.

As Lucy closed the bookstore one evening, she walked through the quiet streets, the distant murmur of protests serving as a haunting backdrop. The American nightmare had taken root, its tendrils winding through the very fabric of society. Lucy couldn't escape the feeling that the nation was hurtling towards a precipice, and the consequences of the fall would reshape the course of history.

In her quiet moments, Lucy found herself reflecting on the fragility of democracy. The system, designed to weather storms and reflect the will of the people, now faced a test that strained its very foundations. The allegations, once whispers in the corridors of power, had grown into a deafening roar that threatened to drown out the ideals that had guided the nation for centuries.

As the night settled over Millington, Lucy stood on the porch of her home, gazing at the stars overhead. The same stars that had witnessed the birth of a nation now bore witness to its struggle for survival. The American nightmare, fueled by allegations and division, cast a shadow that seemed to stretch beyond the town's borders, reaching into the very soul of the nation.

Streets Aflame

The town of Millington, once characterized by its quaint charm, now stood at the epicenter of a storm. The allegations that had rocked the foundations of democracy continued to reverberate through the community, fracturing the unity that had once defined the town. As Lucy Rodriguez navigated the streets, she could feel the tension thick in the air, an invisible force shaping the narrative of a town on the brink.

The morning sun struggled to break through the heavy clouds that hung low over Millington. Lucy, walking to her bookstore, noticed the boarded-up windows of a nearby store, a stark reminder of the protests that had escalated into violence the night before. The town square, which had been a gathering place for celebrations and civic discourse, now bore scars of a community in turmoil.

Inside the bookstore, Lucy found a small group of patrons gathered around a table, their voices lowered in hushed conversation. The headlines of the morning paper spoke of clashes between protesters and law enforcement, and the images depicted a town transformed.

John Mitchell, who had been a regular visitor to the bookstore, approached Lucy with a troubled expression. "Lucy, have you seen the news? It's like the whole town is unraveling."

She nodded, a heavy sigh escaping her. "It's disheartening, John. We were a community bound by shared values, and now… it feels like we're strangers to one another."

As the day unfolded, Lucy observed the changing dynamics in the town. The protests that had initially been a call for transparency and accountability had taken a darker turn. Anger, frustration, and a sense of disillusionment fueled the unrest that spilled onto the streets.

That afternoon, Lucy walked to the town square, the remnants of the previous night's chaos still evident. Broken glass crunched beneath her shoes, and the graffiti that marred the walls seemed to mirror the graffiti that now marked the soul of the community. The American nightmare had manifested itself in the very fabric of Millington.

At the heart of the square, a makeshift memorial had been created for those who had been injured in the clashes. Candles flickered in the afternoon breeze, and the faces of those who had become casualties in a battle for democracy stared back from photographs. The weight of the moment hung heavy, a reminder that the cost of chaos was measured in human lives.

A small group of protesters had gathered near the memorial, their chants echoing through the town. The atmosphere was charged, and as Lucy observed from a distance, she could sense the collective frustration of those who believed their voices had been drowned out by the cacophony of the allegations and the subsequent unrest.

Michael Donovan, the charismatic leader who had emerged as a focal point of the dissent, addressed the crowd. His words were a rallying cry for change, a call to arms against a system that many felt had failed them.

"We won't be silenced!" Michael declared, his voice resonating through the square. "Our demands for justice and transparency will not be ignored. This is a fight for the soul of our town, for the soul of our nation!"

The crowd responded with a fervor that seemed to transcend the immediate issues at hand. It was a collective expression of the frustrations that had simmered beneath the surface for years, now unleashed in the form of a rallying cry against perceived injustice.

Lucy, standing on the outskirts of the gathering, observed the faces of the protesters. They were not faceless agitators but members of her community, people she had known for years. The American nightmare had taken the familiar faces of neighbors and transformed them into participants in a struggle that seemed to have no clear resolution.

As the sun dipped below the horizon, the town square became a stage for a complex drama of conflicting emotions. Protesters clashed with law enforcement, the air thick with tear gas and the shouts of those demanding change. The very streets that had once hosted parades and celebrations now bore witness to a different kind of spectacle—one of unrest, frustration, and the raw, unbridled energy of a community on the edge.

That night, as Lucy closed the bookstore early, she could hear the distant sounds of sirens and the intermittent shouts that echoed through the town. The night had become a canvas for the expression of discontent, and the once-cozy streets of Millington felt like a battleground in a war whose origins were as elusive as its resolution.

The following days saw a further escalation of tensions. The town became a patchwork of conflicting ideologies, with some residents supporting the protests as a necessary expression of frustration, while others decried the violence as a betrayal of the community's values. The fractures that had initially been confined to the realm of politics now seeped into every facet of daily life.

Lucy's bookstore, once a refuge for discourse and the exchange of ideas, became a microcosm of the town's divisions. Patrons engaged in heated debates, their voices rising and falling like the tide of unrest that swept through the streets outside. The very act of civil conversation, it seemed, had become a casualty of the American nightmare.

One afternoon, as Lucy organized the shelves, she overheard a conversation between two customers, a husband and wife whose differences had become emblematic of the wider divide.

"I just can't believe you support these protests," the husband exclaimed, frustration etched on his face. "They're tearing the town apart!"

His wife, her expression equally impassioned, responded, "We can't just sit back and pretend everything is fine. There are real issues that need to be addressed, and this is the only way to make our voices heard."

The exchange, while not uncommon in recent days, left Lucy with a sense of sorrow. The community, once united by a shared sense of identity, now grappled with a rift that seemed to grow wider with each passing conflict.

One evening, Lucy attended a town hall meeting, where residents voiced their concerns and grievances. The meeting, which was intended to be a forum for open dialogue, became a battleground of clashing ideologies. The very institution meant to represent the will of the people now mirrored the divisions that plagued the nation at large.

As Michael Donovan, the charismatic leader of the protests, took the stage, the room buzzed with a mix of anticipation and skepticism. His words, delivered with a fervor that had become characteristic of his public appearances, struck a chord with some and ignited resentment in others.

"We won't back down!" Michael declared, his voice echoing through the hall.

"This town deserves better, and we won't rest until justice is served."

The responses from the audience were varied, reflecting the diversity of perspectives within the community. Some applauded, while others heckled and shouted in dissent. Lucy, seated in the back, observed the scene with a heavy heart. The ideals that had once bound the community were now the battleground on which its future was being determined.

The town's leaders, grappling with the unprecedented challenges, struggled to find a path forward. Calls for unity seemed hollow against the backdrop of streets aflame and a community torn apart. The very essence of Millington seemed to hang in the balance, its fate uncertain in the face of a storm that showed no signs of abating.

Lucy continued to walk through the streets, the echoes of unrest becoming a constant companion. The town, which had once been a haven, now felt like a labyrinth of conflicting emotions. The American nightmare, born out of allegations and the subsequent unrest, had transformed the familiar landscape into uncharted territory.

One night, as Lucy stood on the porch of her home, gazing at the flickering streetlights, a profound sense of grief washed over her. The town, with its charming streets and familiar faces, had become a casualty of the turmoil that gripped the nation. The very idea of community, once a source of strength, now seemed like a distant memory.

In the quiet of the night, Lucy closed her eyes, hoping for a reprieve from the relentless storm. The streets below, once filled with the laughter of children and the footsteps of neighbors, now echoed with a discordant symphony of unrest. The American nightmare, it seemed, had taken root in the very heart of Millington, and Lucy couldn't shake the feeling that the worst was yet to come.

The Rise of a Leader

As Millington grappled with the aftermath of protests and the fractures within the community, a new figure emerged from the shadows, seizing the opportunity to fill the void left by the faltering institutions. This enigmatic leader, whose rise mirrored the chaos that had enveloped the town, captivated the imagination of those desperate for stability and direction.

Lucy Rodriguez, still navigating the turbulent currents of her community, couldn't help but feel a sense of foreboding as she observed the growing influence of this charismatic figure. The town, weary from weeks of unrest, found itself at a crossroads, and the leader who stepped forward promised a return to order and a resolution to the chaos that had gripped Millington.

One morning, as Lucy opened her bookstore, she noticed a gathering in the town square. A podium had been set up, and a large banner hung behind it, displaying a slogan that promised strength and stability. The speaker, a figure draped in confidence, addressed the growing crowd with a voice that carried authority.

"Good citizens of Millington," the leader proclaimed, "I stand before you not as a savior, but as a servant of the community. The chaos that has befallen our town is a call to action, a call to restore order and reclaim the values that bind us together."

Lucy, intrigued and wary in equal measure, joined the onlookers as the leader continued to speak. The rhetoric was a blend of reassurance and determination, and the promises made resonated with those who had grown disillusioned with the uncertainty that had plagued the town.

As the crowd swelled, the leader outlined a vision for Millington that promised security, prosperity, and a return to the tranquil community it once was. The promise of swift action and decisive leadership struck a chord with many, and the leader's charisma seemed to bridge the divides that had fractured the town.

In the days that followed, the leader's influence spread like wildfire. Campaign posters adorned the streets, displaying a face that had quickly become synonymous with the promise of a new beginning. Lucy, still grappling with the complexities of the town's situation, observed the unfolding events with a mix of curiosity and concern.

Michael Donovan, the charismatic leader of the protests, found himself overshadowed by the newcomer. The town's dynamics shifted as supporters of the protests faced a choice between the idealistic promises of change and the allure of a leader who promised order in the face of chaos.

One evening, Lucy attended a town hall meeting where the leader addressed the community. The atmosphere was charged, and the room buzzed with anticipation. The leader's speech, punctuated by applause and nods of agreement, painted a vision of a Millington reborn from the ashes of discord.

"We will not be a town divided," the leader declared, their words resonating through the hall. "We are a community bound by shared values, and together, we will rebuild what has been torn apart."

The promises made were both grand and specific—economic revitalization, a crackdown on crime, and a return to the peaceful coexistence that had once defined Millington. The leader's rhetoric tapped into the collective desire for a return to normalcy, and the town, weary from weeks of unrest, seemed ready to embrace the change promised by this newfound figure.

Lucy, skeptical of the rapid ascent, couldn't shake the feeling that there was more to the leader than met the eye. The promises, while alluring, seemed too good to be true, and the speed at which the leader had gained popularity raised questions about their intentions.

The leader's influence extended beyond speeches and promises. Community initiatives were launched, aimed at restoring a sense of pride and unity. Cleanup campaigns, economic development projects, and outreach programs became the tools through which the leader sought to reshape the town's narrative.

As Lucy walked through the streets, she noticed the subtle changes—the freshly painted walls, the organized community events, and the growing sense of optimism among those who embraced the leader's vision. The town, it seemed, was on the cusp of a transformation, and the leader's popularity soared with each passing day.

However, not everyone was swept up by the wave of optimism. Some residents, still skeptical of the leader's intentions, questioned the rapid changes and the erosion of democratic processes. The town's diversity of opinions now found expression in whispered conversations, as friends and neighbors grappled with the implications of a leader whose rise seemed too convenient in the midst of chaos.

Lucy found herself caught between the optimism of those who saw the leader as a beacon of hope and the skepticism of those who feared the consequences of blind allegiance. The community, already fractured, now faced a new division—one defined by allegiance to the charismatic figure who promised a return to order.

One evening, as Lucy closed the bookstore, she encountered Emma Thompson, who had been an active participant in the earlier protests. Emma's expression conveyed a mix of curiosity and doubt as she spoke.

"Lucy, have you noticed how quickly things are changing? It's like the leader has a plan for everything. But is it too good to be true?"

Lucy nodded, sharing Emma's concerns. "It's important to question, Emma. Change is inevitable, but we must ensure it aligns with the values that define our community. Blind trust can lead to unintended consequences."

As the leader's influence solidified, the town's institutions underwent a transformation. Those who had been critical of the leader's rise found themselves marginalized, their voices drowned out by the growing chorus of support. The leader's inner circle, a group of advisors and allies, became the architects of the town's new direction.

The local newspaper, once a platform for diverse voices, now carried headlines that echoed the leader's narrative. Dissent, it seemed, was not tolerated in the pursuit of the promised stability. Lucy, reading the articles with a sense of unease, couldn't shake the feeling that the very essence of democracy was being eroded in the name of order.

One afternoon, as Lucy walked through the town square, she encountered Mr. Johnson, the war veteran. His expression, usually a portrait of resilience, now bore traces of concern.

"Lucy," he said, his voice lowered, "this leader—there's an air of authoritarianism in the way they operate. We must tread carefully. Democracy is a delicate balance, and we can't afford to sacrifice it for the illusion of stability."

Lucy nodded in agreement, grateful for the wisdom of someone who had witnessed the consequences of unchecked power. The warnings of a fragile democracy lingered in the air as the town moved forward, seemingly on the precipice of a new era.

The leader's popularity, despite the concerns raised by some, reached new heights. Campaign rallies, once a hallmark of political campaigns, now became showcases of the leader's influence. The town, under the spell of a vision promised, appeared willing to embrace the leader as the architect of its future.

One evening, Lucy attended a rally in the town square, where the leader addressed the community. The atmosphere was electric, the crowd hanging onto every word spoken from the podium. The promises of stability, economic growth, and a return to the values that defined the community resonated with the audience.

As Lucy stood among the sea of faces, she couldn't help but feel a sense of disquiet. The leader's rise had been meteoric, and the fervor with which they were embraced hinted at the deep yearning for a return to normalcy. Yet, in the pursuit of stability, Lucy wondered if the town was sacrificing the very principles that had once made it a beacon of community.

The leader's speech reached its climax, and the crowd erupted into cheers. The vision promised seemed within reach, and the town, it appeared, was ready to embark on a new chapter under the guidance of its charismatic leader.

In the aftermath of the rally, Lucy walked through the now eerily quiet streets. The cheers still echoed in her mind, but beneath the surface, a nagging doubt persisted. The leader, with their promises of stability, had captured the imagination of a town desperate for direction. However, Lucy couldn't shake the feeling that the rise of this charismatic figure marked not the end of the American nightmare, but a new chapter—one with consequences that remained unseen.

As she entered her home, Lucy gazed out of the window, the night sky stretching above. The stars, silent witnesses to the town's evolution, seemed to hold the secrets of a future yet to unfold. The American nightmare, born out of allegations and unrest, had taken a new form—one that walked the streets of Millington with a confidence that both intrigued and unsettled. Lucy closed her eyes, bracing herself for the uncertainties that lay ahead, aware that the town's journey had taken an unexpected turn, guided by the hand of a leader whose influence would shape its destiny.

Unraveling Threads

The days that followed the leader's ascent saw Millington undergoing a transformation, the echoes of the recent protests now replaced by a carefully curated narrative of stability and progress. Lucy Rodriguez, ever watchful, observed as the leader's vision unfolded, reshaping the town in ways that both intrigued and unnerved its residents.

The morning sun painted the streets of Millington with a warm glow, but the atmosphere carried a tension that lingered beneath the surface. Lucy, walking through the town square, noticed the changes that marked the new era—the meticulous flower beds that replaced the remnants of protest graffiti, the banners heralding economic revitalization, and the palpable sense of order that now defined the once chaotic heart of the community.

The leader's promises were manifesting in tangible ways. Economic development projects, seemingly materializing overnight, aimed to breathe life into the town's struggling businesses. The streets buzzed with activity as workers painted facades, repaired sidewalks, and planted flowers in an orchestrated effort to rejuvenate Millington's image.

As Lucy entered her bookstore, she couldn't escape the sense of dissonance between the curated facade of progress and the underlying questions that still lingered in the minds of some residents. The leader's rise, marked by promises of stability, seemed to be erasing the scars of recent turmoil, but Lucy couldn't shake the feeling that the town was walking a delicate tightrope between order and the erosion of democratic principles.

The local newspaper, once a platform for diverse opinions, now carried headlines that painted a rosy picture of the town's revival under the leader's guidance. Dissent, if it existed, was relegated to the fringes, the voices of those wary of the rapid changes drowned out by the orchestrated narrative of progress.

One afternoon, Lucy attended a community event organized by the leader's team. The town square, adorned with banners celebrating the "Millington Renaissance," bustled with residents eager to witness the tangible fruits of the promised revitalization. The leader, flanked by advisors and allies, spoke from a stage adorned with symbols of the town's new direction.

"We stand at the threshold of a new era for Millington," the leader declared, their voice carrying across the square. "Together, we will build a community that stands as a beacon of prosperity and unity."

The crowd erupted into applause, their enthusiasm palpable. Lucy, standing among the onlookers, sensed the genuine hope that the leader's words inspired. The desire for a better future was universal, and in that shared yearning, the town found a semblance of unity.

The leader's initiatives extended beyond cosmetic changes. Town hall meetings, once a forum for open dialogue, now became orchestrated events where questions were carefully vetted, and responses adhered to the prescribed narrative of progress. The very essence of democracy, Lucy noted, was undergoing a subtle transformation—one that raised questions about the true nature of the stability promised.

One evening, as Lucy closed the bookstore, she encountered Emma Thompson, whose expression conveyed a mixture of curiosity and concern.

"Lucy, have you noticed how tightly controlled everything is now? It's like we're living in a carefully crafted story, and I can't help but wonder if there's more going on behind the scenes."

Lucy nodded in agreement. "Emma, the facade of progress is undeniable, but we must remain vigilant. Democracy thrives on transparency and open discourse. We can't allow the appearance of stability to mask the erosion of our principles."

As the weeks passed, Millington became a town of contrasts. The revitalized streets, once marked by protests, now showcased the vision of the leader's team. However, beneath the surface, a sense of unease simmered among those who questioned the true motives behind the rapid changes.

The leader's influence extended into every aspect of the town's life. Educational curricula were adjusted to reflect the narrative of the Millington Renaissance, and institutions that had once prided themselves on academic freedom now operated within the confines of the prescribed ideology. Lucy, a staunch advocate for the power of education, couldn't help but feel a pang of concern for the erosion of intellectual diversity.

One day, Lucy received a visit from John Mitchell, the history teacher, who had long been a vocal advocate for open discourse and critical thinking. His expression, a mixture of frustration and resignation, hinted at the challenges faced by those who questioned the new order.

"Lucy," John sighed, "it's getting harder to teach the principles of democracy when the very institution of education is being molded to fit a specific narrative. How do we preserve the essence of learning when the truth is being carefully curated?"

Lucy, sympathetic to John's concerns, pondered the challenges faced by educators in a town undergoing a profound transformation. The unraveling threads of democracy seemed to weave through every facet of Millington's existence, and the consequences of this quiet erosion were becoming increasingly apparent.

Despite the carefully cultivated image of stability, signs of dissent began to surface. Small gatherings, held in private spaces, became forums for those who questioned the direction the town was taking. Lucy, ever attuned to the pulse of the community, attended one such gathering in the backroom of a local cafe.

The participants, a diverse group of residents, voiced concerns about the rapid changes and the lack of transparency in decision-making. The leader's promises, while alluring, seemed to be veiling a more complex reality—one that raised questions about the preservation of individual freedoms and democratic principles.

Michael Donovan, the charismatic leader of the earlier protests, emerged as a voice of dissent within this clandestine gathering. His words carried a weight born out of experience, and he warned of the dangers of trading the ideals of democracy for the illusion of stability.

"We can't allow the town we love to become a puppet in the hands of those who seek to control the narrative," Michael asserted. "True progress can only be achieved through open dialogue and the inclusion of diverse perspectives."

As Lucy listened to the discussions, she couldn't help but feel a glimmer of hope. The unraveling threads of dissent, carefully woven in the shadows, suggested that the spirit of democracy had not been entirely extinguished. The town, it seemed, harbored a resilience that transcended the curated image of stability.

The leader, perhaps sensing the undercurrents of dissent, responded with a renewed vigor. Public appearances and speeches became more frequent, the narrative of progress more emphatic. Lucy observed the town square, now adorned with banners proclaiming the success of the Millington Renaissance, and wondered if the surface-level transformations were enough to quell the deeper questions that lingered in the hearts of some residents.

One evening, as Lucy walked through the streets, she encountered Emma Thompson, who appeared troubled by a realization.

"Lucy, it's like we're living in a gilded cage. Yes, there's order and progress, but at what cost? Are we sacrificing our freedom for the illusion of stability?"

Lucy, empathizing with Emma's concerns, pondered the delicate balance between order and the preservation of democratic principles. The American nightmare, it seemed, had taken on a new form—one that hid behind the veneer of progress while quietly unraveling the threads that bound the community together.

As the town approached a pivotal moment, Lucy couldn't escape the feeling that the true consequences of the leader's influence were yet to unfold. The streets of Millington, once marked by protests, now bore witness to a different kind of unrest—an internal conflict that pitted the desire for stability against the imperceptible erosion of the very principles that had defined the town for generations.

In her quiet moments, Lucy found herself reflecting on the fragility of democracy. The American nightmare, born out of allegations and chaos, seemed to have taken a new form—one that challenged the town to confront its values and grapple with the consequences of a path chosen in the pursuit of a seemingly elusive stability.

The nights in Millington, once defined by the quiet hum of a close-knit community, now held a different kind of silence. It was the silence of uncertainty, the quiet unraveling of threads that had woven the fabric of the town for centuries. As Lucy closed her eyes, bracing herself for the challenges yet to come, she couldn't shake the feeling that the true test of Millington's resilience lay ahead, in the shadows where dissent lingered and the echoes of the American nightmare reverberated through the quiet streets.

Whispers of Rebellion

As Millington continued to navigate the delicate balance between the illusion of stability and the erosion of democratic principles, whispers of rebellion permeated the air. The town, once defined by its close-knit community, now grappled with a growing undercurrent of dissent that simmered beneath the surface. Lucy Rodriguez, ever attuned to the pulse of the community, found herself drawn into the shadows where the voices of those questioning the status quo were beginning to coalesce.

The morning sun cast long shadows through the streets as Lucy made her way to the bookstore. The town square, adorned with banners proclaiming the Millington Renaissance, seemed to gleam in the sunlight. However, the atmosphere carried a tension that hinted at the growing disquiet beneath the surface.

Inside the bookstore, Lucy noticed an increased hush among the patrons. Conversations, once animated, now took on a cautious tone as if the very act of speaking freely had become a risky endeavor. The leader's influence, omnipresent in every corner of the town, cast a shadow that seemed to stifle open discourse.

John Mitchell, the history teacher, approached Lucy with a sense of urgency. "Lucy, we need to talk. The school—there are changes happening, and not for the better. Academic freedom is being sacrificed for the sake of a prescribed narrative."

Lucy, troubled by the implications, listened as John described the subtle shifts in the educational landscape. The curriculum, once a platform for critical thinking, now adhered to a narrative that celebrated the leader's vision while sidelining perspectives that deviated from the prescribed ideology.

"This isn't education; it's indoctrination," John lamented. "Our students deserve better, and we can't allow the erosion of intellectual diversity in the pursuit of a false stability."

The concerns raised by John mirrored the growing unease among those who refused to conform to the narrative of progress. As Lucy walked through the town, she noticed small gatherings in hidden corners—a cafe backroom, a secluded park bench—where residents exchanged furtive glances and spoke in hushed tones.

One evening, Lucy attended one of these clandestine meetings. The group, a diverse collection of residents who had once been united by a shared love for their town, now found common ground in their shared concern for the erosion of democratic principles.

Emma Thompson, whose skepticism had grown in the face of the town's transformation, spoke passionately. "We can't allow fear to silence us. Millington deserves a future built on openness, not on the suppression of dissent. It's time to reclaim the essence of our community."

Michael Donovan, the charismatic figure who had led protests in the earlier days, echoed Emma's sentiments. "We've seen the consequences of blind allegiance. It's our duty to question, to ensure that the path we tread is one that aligns with the values we hold dear."

The group, though small in number, represented a cross-section of Millington's population. Teachers, small business owners, students, and retirees— each contributing to the mosaic of perspectives that had once defined the town. The whispers of rebellion, it seemed, were not confined to the shadows but were gaining strength as a collective murmur of discontent.

As Lucy listened to the discussions, she couldn't help but feel a glimmer of hope. The town, once unified in its shared values, was grappling with the complexities of change. The challenge, she realized, lay not only in questioning the current trajectory but in proposing an alternative vision that could unite the diverse voices within Millington.

In the following days, the whispers of rebellion evolved into a more organized effort. The group, now calling themselves the "Guardians of Democracy," sought to reclaim the spaces where open discourse had once thrived. They distributed pamphlets, organized community forums, and engaged in quiet acts of resistance aimed at challenging the carefully curated narrative that had taken root in the town.

Lucy, drawn into the efforts of the Guardians, found herself at the center of a movement that aimed to preserve the very principles that had defined Millington for generations. The bookstore, once a sanctuary for the exchange of ideas, became a meeting place for those who refused to be silenced.

One afternoon, as Lucy organized a community forum, she encountered Mr. Johnson, the war veteran, who had been observing the town's transformation with a sense of growing concern.

"Lucy, the town we fought for—the town that stood as a symbol of freedom and resilience—is slipping away. We can't allow the sacrifice of those who came before us to be in vain."

Lucy nodded, recognizing the weight of Mr. Johnson's words. The Guardians of Democracy, she realized, were not just resisting for the sake of resistance but were fighting to reclaim the soul of a community that had been veering off course.

The forum, held in the town square under the watchful gaze of banners celebrating the Millington Renaissance, drew a diverse crowd. Residents, some curious and others cautious, gathered to hear the voices of dissent that challenged the prevailing narrative. The Guardians spoke eloquently, articulating the concerns of those who believed that progress should not come at the expense of democratic values.

Emma Thompson, standing at the forefront, declared, "We're not here to tear down; we're here to build a future that honors our principles. Millington can be a beacon of progress without sacrificing the essence of what makes us a community."

The response from the crowd was mixed. Some, swayed by the carefully crafted narrative of progress, remained skeptical of the Guardians' message. Others, however, listened with a sense of awakening, realizing that the path to true progress required a careful examination of the values that had sustained the town for generations.

In the weeks that followed, the Guardians of Democracy expanded their efforts. The bookstore, once a symbol of resistance, became a hub for organizing events that aimed to reignite the spirit of open discourse. Lucy, at the helm of this quiet rebellion, navigated the delicate balance between challenging the status quo and fostering unity among those who questioned the direction of the town.

The leader, sensing the growing resistance, responded with increased vigilance. The town square, once a space for community events, now bore a heavier police presence, and public gatherings were scrutinized for signs of dissent. The leader's influence extended into every corner of Millington, creating an environment where questioning the prescribed narrative came at a cost.

One evening, as Lucy closed the bookstore, she encountered Emma Thompson, whose determination seemed unwavering despite the challenges they faced.

"Lucy, we can't back down. The town we love is worth fighting for, even if it means challenging those in power. We need to remind everyone that democracy is not a gift to be taken for granted but a responsibility we all share."

Lucy, inspired by Emma's resolve, nodded in agreement. The Guardians of Democracy, she realized, were not just a voice of dissent but a reminder of the principles that had once bound Millington together.

The town, caught between the allure of stability and the whispers of rebellion, stood at a crossroads. The streets, once marked by protests and later adorned with banners celebrating progress, now bore witness to a different kind of conflict—one that played out not in clashes of ideology but in the quiet resistance of those who believed that the soul of Millington was worth preserving.

As Lucy stood on the porch of her home, gazing at the stars overhead, she couldn't escape the feeling that the town's journey was far from over. The American nightmare, born out of allegations and chaos, had taken root in the very heart of Millington. Yet, in the whispers of rebellion, Lucy found a glimmer of hope—a reminder that the values that defined the town were resilient, and that the true test of its character lay not in conformity but in the courage to question, to resist, and to reclaim the essence of democracy that had long defined the spirit of Millington.

The Tipping Point

As Millington grappled with the dueling forces of conformity and dissent, the town found itself on the brink of a tipping point. Lucy Rodriguez, at the center of the quiet rebellion led by the Guardians of Democracy, felt the weight of the town's destiny pressing upon her. The struggle for the soul of Millington intensified, and the choices made in the coming days would shape the narrative of a community torn between the allure of stability and the call of its democratic roots.

The days unfolded with a sense of anticipation, the tension in the air palpable. The town square, once a symbol of unity, had become a battleground of ideas, each gathering and event a subtle assertion of the values that residents held dear.

The Guardians of Democracy, bolstered by a growing wave of support, organized a town hall meeting—an open forum where residents could engage in a meaningful dialogue about the future of Millington. The bookstore, now a rallying point for those who questioned the direction of the town, buzzed with activity as volunteers prepared for the event.

Lucy, surrounded by a dedicated team of residents who believed in the power of open discourse, felt a mixture of hope and trepidation. The town had reached a juncture where the choices made could either steer Millington back toward its democratic principles or plunge it further into the embrace of a carefully curated narrative.

The evening of the town hall arrived, and the square filled with residents eager to participate in the conversation. Banners celebrating the Millington Renaissance hung overhead, casting a shadow over the gathering. The leader, perhaps sensing the threat posed by open dialogue, had authorized a counter-event to showcase the progress achieved under their guidance.

As Lucy took the stage, a hush fell over the crowd. The choice between the two events had become a symbol of the town's internal struggle—whether to adhere to the prescribed narrative or to embrace the diversity of opinions that had long defined Millington.

"Thank you all for being here tonight," Lucy began, her voice carrying a sincerity born out of a deep love for her community. "We stand at a crossroads. Millington is a town rich in history, a history built on the foundations of democracy, freedom, and open dialogue. We must ask ourselves: What kind of town do we want to be?"

The leader's event, just a stone's throw away, boasted a carefully chore-ographed presentation of progress. Economic statistics, testimonials from select community members, and a narrative of stability unfolded on a stage adorned with symbols of the Millington Renaissance. The atmosphere, while celebratory, carried an undercurrent of control—an orchestrated display designed to reaffirm the leader's vision.

Back at the town hall, the Guardians of Democracy took turns addressing the crowd. Emma Thompson, her conviction unwavering, spoke passionately about the importance of preserving the town's democratic values.

"Progress should not come at the cost of our principles. We can build a future that combines stability with the open exchange of ideas. Let Millington be a town where every voice is heard, not just the ones that conform to a predetermined narrative."

Michael Donovan, his charisma a beacon of resistance, added, "Our town is at its best when we celebrate our diversity, when we engage in open dialogue even when it's uncomfortable. Let's not sacrifice the essence of Millington for the illusion of stability."

The town hall meeting evolved into a dynamic exchange of ideas. Residents shared their perspectives, asked tough questions, and expressed a range of emotions—from optimism about the progress showcased by the leader to concerns about the erosion of democratic principles.

Across the square, the leader's event continued with a carefully orchestrated program. Speeches were delivered, accolades were bestowed, and the narrative of progress was reinforced with each carefully chosen word. The contrast between the two gatherings—the open dialogue of the town hall and the controlled presentation of the leader's event—symbolized the internal struggle playing out within Millington.

As the evening progressed, the leader, perhaps sensing the potency of the Guardians of Democracy's message, decided to address the town hall directly. The atmosphere shifted as the leader's entourage approached the stage, their presence a subtle assertion of authority.

"We appreciate the diversity of opinions in our town," the leader began, their words measured. "But progress requires decisive leadership. We have a vision—a vision that ensures stability, prosperity, and a return to the values that define our community."

The leader's words, while confident, failed to quell the questions and concerns raised by the Guardians of Democracy. The town, it seemed, stood at a precipice, torn between the allure of a vision promised and the foundational principles that had sustained Millington for generations.

As the leader spoke, Lucy couldn't shake the feeling that the true test lay not in the words delivered from the stage but in the choices made by the residents in the days to come. The American nightmare, it seemed, had taken root not just in allegations and chaos but in the internal struggle of a community forced to confront its values.

In the days following the town hall, Millington found itself at the center of a growing national conversation. News outlets, drawn by the drama playing out in the town square, descended upon Millington to capture the essence of a community wrestling with its identity.

The leader, seeking to control the narrative, framed the Guardians of Democracy as agitators and dissenters. The town's newspapers, once a platform for diverse voices, now carried headlines that echoed the leader's narrative. Lucy, reading the articles with a sense of unease, couldn't shake the feeling that the battle for the soul of Millington had reached a critical juncture.

The Guardians of Democracy, undeterred by the attempts to marginalize their message, intensified their efforts. Community forums, neighborhood discussions, and outreach initiatives became tools through which they sought to bridge the divides within the town. Lucy, at the forefront of this quiet rebellion, felt the weight of responsibility on her shoulders.

One evening, as Lucy closed the bookstore, she encountered Emma Thompson, whose determination remained unyielding.

"Lucy, we can't let the leader control the narrative. Millington deserves a future built on openness, not on the suppression of dissent. We need to reach every corner of the town and remind our fellow residents of the values that define us."

Lucy, inspired by Emma's resilience, nodded in agreement. The town, she realized, had not yet reached its tipping point. The choices made by its residents in the days to come would determine whether Millington would succumb to the allure of a curated narrative or rise above the challenges to reclaim the essence of democracy.

The leader, sensing the growing influence of the Guardians of Democracy, responded with increased efforts to suppress dissent. The town square, once a symbol of community unity, became a stage for political maneuvering. Police presence intensified, public gatherings were monitored, and dissenting voices were met with subtle forms of intimidation.

Despite the challenges, the Guardians of Democracy pressed on. The bookstore, now a symbol of resistance, continued to serve as a meeting place for those who believed that Millington's future could only be secured through open dialogue and the preservation of democratic values.

One afternoon, as Lucy organized another community forum, she encountered Mr. Johnson, the war veteran, whose eyes reflected a sense of concern and determination.

"Lucy, the battle for democracy is not won in a day. It's a continuous struggle, one that requires resilience and a commitment to the principles that define us. We can't let fear dictate the choices we make."

Lucy, inspired by Mr. Johnson's wisdom, nodded in agreement. The tipping point, she realized, was not a singular moment but a continuous journey—a journey that required the collective strength of a community determined to shape its own destiny.

As the sun dipped below the horizon, casting long shadows through the town square, Lucy gazed at the stars overhead. The night, once a canvas of quiet reflection, now held the weight of a community at a crossroads. The

American nightmare, born out of allegations and chaos, had taken root in Millington, but the struggle for its soul continued.

In the quiet moments before the town slept, Lucy couldn't escape the feeling that the choices made in the days to come would determine not just the fate of Millington but the resilience of democracy itself. The stars, silent witnesses to the town's evolution, seemed to hold the secrets of a future yet to unfold. The tipping point, it seemed, awaited its moment, and Lucy, bracing herself for the challenges ahead, stood ready to face the consequences of a journey that had become a testament to the strength of a community at the crossroads of its destiny.

The Resilience of Community

In the days that followed the pivotal town hall meeting, Millington found itself caught in a swirling tempest of conflicting narratives. The leader, sensing the growing influence of the Guardians of Democracy, responded with increased efforts to control the narrative and suppress dissent. The town, once a haven of community unity, now stood at a crossroads, its residents facing choices that would shape the very fabric of their shared existence. Lucy Rodriguez, a central figure in the quiet rebellion, found herself navigating the storm, torn between the allure of stability and the call of democracy.

The town square, once a symbol of community gatherings, now bore the scars of the internal struggle. Banners celebrating the Millington Renaissance fluttered alongside a growing number of posters and signs expressing diverse opinions. The atmosphere carried a tension that had become palpable, the collective heartbeat of a town at a critical juncture.

Lucy, undeterred by the challenges that lay ahead, continued to organize community forums and events. The bookstore, now a sanctuary for open dialogue, became a refuge for residents seeking a space to voice their concerns. The Guardians of Democracy, their ranks swelling with diverse voices, pressed on with their mission to bridge the divides within Millington.

One evening, as Lucy walked through the town square, she encountered Emma Thompson, whose determination remained unyielding despite the challenges they faced.

"Lucy, the leader's influence is growing, but so is our movement. We can't let fear dictate our actions. Millington deserves a future built on openness, not on the suppression of dissent."

Lucy, inspired by Emma's resilience, nodded in agreement. The battle for the soul of Millington was far from over, and the choices made by its residents in the coming days would determine whether the town would succumb to the allure of a curated narrative or rise above the challenges to reclaim the essence of democracy.

The leader, aware of the growing influence of the Guardians of Democracy, sought to further tighten their grip on the town's narrative. Police presence in the town square increased, public gatherings were scrutinized, and dissenting voices faced subtle forms of intimidation. The leader's message, reinforced through controlled media narratives, aimed to create a perception of stability even as the foundations of democracy trembled.

Despite the challenges, the Guardians of Democracy expanded their efforts. Small gatherings in neighborhoods became forums for open dialogue, where residents could express their concerns away from the watchful eyes of authority. The movement, fueled by a shared commitment to democratic values, began to permeate every corner of Millington.

One afternoon, as Lucy organized another community forum, she encountered John Mitchell, the history teacher, whose determination to preserve the essence of education mirrored the broader struggle within the town.

"Lucy, the battle we're facing is not just about the town square; it's about the very classrooms where ideas are cultivated. We can't allow education to become a tool for indoctrination. Our students deserve better."

Lucy, sympathetic to John's concerns, acknowledged the vital role education played in shaping the future of Millington. The unraveling threads of democracy, she realized, were woven not just in public spaces but in the institutions that had long defined the town's character.

As the weeks passed, Millington became a town of contrasts. The leader's influence, marked by controlled narratives and a carefully orchestrated vision of progress, coexisted with the growing undercurrent of dissent fostered by the Guardians of Democracy. The bookstore, now a symbol of resistance, became a beacon for those seeking refuge from the stifling atmosphere outside.

One evening, Lucy received a visit from Michael Donovan, whose charismatic presence had been a guiding force in the earlier protests. His eyes reflected a sense of urgency.

"Lucy, the town square is not enough. We need to reach every neighborhood, every corner where the leader's influence has taken root. Our movement must be a reflection of the diversity that defines Millington."

Lucy, recognizing the truth in Michael's words, joined forces with the Guardians of Democracy to expand their outreach. Neighborhood gatherings, town hall meetings in various districts, and small discussions in local businesses became the channels through which the movement sought to rekindle the spirit of open dialogue.

The leader, perhaps sensing the growing resilience of the community, responded with increased efforts to suppress dissent. The town square, once a space for community unity, became a stage for political maneuvering. The police presence intensified, public gatherings were monitored, and those associated with the Guardians of Democracy faced subtle forms of intimidation.

In the face of adversity, Lucy found herself reflecting on the resilience of community. The American nightmare, born out of allegations and chaos, had taken root in Millington, but the spirit of its residents refused to be extinguished. The unraveling threads of democracy, she realized, were not a sign of weakness but a testament to the strength of a community determined to shape its own destiny.

One day, as Lucy walked through the streets, she encountered Mr. Johnson, the war veteran, whose expression conveyed a mixture of concern and determination.

"Lucy, the battle we're facing is not just about the present; it's about the legacy we leave for future generations. We can't allow fear to dictate our choices. The soul of Millington is worth fighting for."

Lucy, inspired by Mr. Johnson's words, nodded in agreement. The town, she realized, stood at a tipping point—a moment where the choices made would define not just the trajectory of Millington but the resilience of democracy itself.

As the weeks unfolded, the struggle within Millington intensified. The leader, seeking to tighten their grip on the narrative, escalated efforts to suppress dissent. The Guardians of Democracy, fueled by a collective determination, expanded their outreach, reaching every neighborhood, every corner where the leader's influence had taken root.

One evening, as Lucy closed the bookstore, she encountered Emma Thompson, whose eyes reflected a mixture of exhaustion and hope.

"Lucy, the town is weary, but we can't give up. The spirit of Millington is alive in every voice that refuses to be silenced. We need to remind everyone that democracy is not a gift but a responsibility we all share."

Lucy, inspired by Emma's resilience, nodded in agreement. The American nightmare, it seemed, had not broken the spirit of Millington but had ignited a flame of determination within its residents. The choices made in the coming days, she realized, would determine not just the fate of the town but the legacy it would leave for generations to come.

The town square, once a symbol of unity, now bore witness to a different kind of conflict. Banners celebrating progress hung alongside signs expressing diverse opinions. The police presence, a silent reminder of authority, coexisted with the growing resilience of a community unwilling to surrender its democratic principles.

One evening, as Lucy stood on the stage in the town square, addressing a diverse crowd that had gathered for a community forum, she felt the weight of responsibility on her shoulders. The American nightmare, born out of allegations and chaos, had taken root in Millington, but the struggle for its soul had become a beacon of hope for communities across the nation.

"Millington," Lucy began, her voice carrying the collective heartbeat of the town, "we stand at a crossroads. The choices we make in the coming days will define the future of our community. Let us not be swayed by fear or the allure of a curated narrative. Instead, let us embrace the diversity of opinions that has long defined us.

The soul of Millington is resilient, and together, we can navigate the storm and emerge stronger on the other side."

The crowd, a mosaic of faces reflecting the diversity of Millington, listened with a sense of introspection. The unraveling threads of democracy, Lucy realized, were not a sign of defeat but a call to action—a reminder that the strength of a community lay not in conformity but in the collective courage to question, to resist, and to reclaim the essence of democracy.

As Lucy closed her eyes, bracing herself for the challenges yet to come, she couldn't escape the feeling that the true test of Millington's resilience lay ahead. The town, caught between the allure of stability and the whispers of rebellion, stood at a crossroads where the choices made would echo through the corridors of history. The American nightmare, it seemed, had become a battleground for the very soul of a community determined to shape its own destiny.

Echoes of Democracy

As Millington navigated the tumultuous landscape of conflicting narratives and internal strife, the town found itself on the cusp of a defining moment. Lucy Rodriguez, a central figure in the quiet rebellion led by the Guardians of Democracy, felt the weight of the community's destiny pressing upon her. The struggle for the soul of Millington had become a beacon of hope for communities across the nation, a microcosm of the larger battle between the allure of stability and the call of democracy.

The town square, once a symbol of unity, now stood as a stage for the clash of ideas. Banners proclaiming progress mingled with signs expressing diverse opinions, creating a visual cacophony that mirrored the internal conflict within Millington. The leader's influence, marked by controlled narratives and a carefully curated vision of progress, coexisted with the growing resilience of a community unwilling to surrender its democratic principles.

In the days following the pivotal town hall meeting, Millington had become a town of contrasts. The leader, aware of the growing influence of the Guardians of Democracy, responded with increased efforts to control the narrative and suppress dissent. Police presence in the town square intensified, public gatherings were monitored, and dissenting voices faced subtle forms of intimidation.

Despite the challenges, the Guardians of Democracy pressed on. The bookstore, now a symbol of resistance, continued to serve as a meeting place for residents seeking refuge from the stifling atmosphere outside. Community forums, neighborhood discussions, and outreach initiatives became tools through which the movement sought to rekindle the spirit of open dialogue.

One afternoon, as Lucy organized another community forum, she encountered Emma Thompson, whose eyes reflected a mixture of exhaustion and determination.

"Lucy, the town is weary, but we can't give up. The spirit of Millington is alive in every voice that refuses to be silenced. We need to remind everyone that democracy is not a gift but a responsibility we all share."

Lucy, inspired by Emma's resilience, nodded in agreement. The American nightmare, it seemed, had not broken the spirit of Millington but had ignited a flame of determination within its residents. The choices made in the coming days, she realized, would determine not just the fate of the town but the legacy it would leave for generations to come.

In the weeks that followed, Millington became a town in flux. The leader, seeking to tighten their grip on the narrative, escalated efforts to suppress dissent. The Guardians of Democracy, fueled by a collective determination, expanded their outreach, reaching every neighborhood, every corner where the leader's influence had taken root.

One evening, as Lucy closed the bookstore, she encountered Michael Donovan, whose charismatic presence had been a guiding force in the earlier protests. His eyes reflected a sense of urgency.

"Lucy, the town square is not enough. We need to reach every neighborhood, every corner where the leader's influence has taken root. Our movement must be a reflection of the diversity that defines Millington."

Lucy, recognizing the truth in Michael's words, joined forces with the Guardians of Democracy to expand their outreach. Neighborhood gatherings, town hall meetings in various districts, and small discussions in local businesses became the channels through which the movement sought to rekindle the spirit of open dialogue.

The leader, perhaps sensing the growing resilience of the community, responded with increased efforts to suppress dissent. The town square, once a space for community unity, became a stage for political maneuvering. The police presence intensified, public gatherings were monitored, and those associated with the Guardians of Democracy faced subtle forms of intimidation.

In the face of adversity, Lucy found herself reflecting on the resilience of community. The American nightmare, born out of allegations and chaos, had taken root in Millington, but the spirit of its residents refused to be extinguished. The unraveling threads of democracy, she realized, were not a sign of weakness but a testament to the strength of a community determined to shape its own destiny.

One day, as Lucy walked through the streets, she encountered Mr. Johnson, the war veteran, whose expression conveyed a mixture of concern and determination.

"Lucy, the battle we're facing is not just about the present; it's about the legacy we leave for future generations. We can't allow fear to dictate our choices. The soul of Millington is worth fighting for."

Lucy, inspired by Mr. Johnson's words, nodded in agreement. The town, she realized, stood at a tipping point—a moment where the choices made would define not just the trajectory of Millington but the resilience of democracy itself.

As the weeks unfolded, the struggle within Millington intensified. The leader, seeking to tighten their grip on the narrative, escalated efforts to suppress dissent. The Guardians of Democracy, fueled by a collective determination, expanded their outreach, reaching every neighborhood, every corner where the leader's influence had taken root.

One evening, as Lucy closed the bookstore, she encountered Emma Thompson, whose eyes reflected a mixture of exhaustion and hope.

"Lucy, the town is weary, but we can't give up. The spirit of Millington is alive in every voice that refuses to be silenced. We need to remind everyone that democracy is not a gift but a responsibility we all share."

Lucy, inspired by Emma's resilience, nodded in agreement. The American nightmare, it seemed, had not broken the spirit of Millington but had ignited a flame of determination within its residents. The choices made in the coming days, she realized, would determine not just the fate of the town but the legacy it would leave for generations to come.

The town square, once a symbol of unity, now bore witness to a different kind of conflict. Banners celebrating progress hung alongside signs expressing diverse opinions. The police presence, a silent reminder of authority, coexisted with the growing resilience of a community unwilling to surrender its democratic principles.

One evening, as Lucy stood on the stage in the town square, addressing a diverse crowd that had gathered for a community forum, she felt the weight of responsibility on her shoulders. The American nightmare, born out of allegations and chaos, had taken root in Millington, but the struggle for its soul had become a beacon of hope for communities across the nation.

"Millington," Lucy began, her voice carrying the collective heartbeat of the town, "we stand at a crossroads. The choices we make in the coming days will define the future of our community. Let us not be swayed by fear or the allure of a curated narrative. Instead, let us embrace the diversity of opinions that has long defined us. The soul of Millington is resilient, and together, we can navigate the storm and emerge stronger on the other side."

The crowd, a mosaic of faces reflecting the diversity of Millington, listened with a sense of introspection. The unraveling threads of democracy, Lucy realized, were not a sign of defeat but a call to action—a reminder that the strength of a community lay not in conformity but in the collective courage to question, to resist, and to reclaim the essence of democracy.

As Lucy closed her eyes, bracing herself for the challenges yet to come, she couldn't escape the feeling that the true test of Millington's resilience lay ahead. The town, caught between the allure of stability and the whispers of rebellion, stood at a crossroads where the choices made would echo through the corridors of history. The American nightmare, it seemed, had become a battleground for the very soul of a community determined to shape its own destiny.

In the quiet moments before the town slept, Lucy couldn't help but reflect on the journey that had brought Millington to this point. The choices made by its residents, she realized, were not just a reflection of the present but a legacy that would endure in the annals of history. The American nightmare, born out of allegations and chaos, had become a catalyst for a movement that transcended the boundaries of one town and resonated with the collective yearning for a future built on the principles that defined a nation.

As Lucy gazed at the stars overhead, she found solace in their silent witness to the struggles and triumphs of a community at the crossroads. The echoes of democracy, she believed, would endure, carried forward by the voices of those who refused to be silenced. The journey, she knew, was far from over, but the resilience of Millington, illuminated by the quiet glow of determination, held the promise of a future where the true spirit of democracy would prevail.

The Heartbeat of Rebellion

As Millington weathered the storm of conflicting ideologies, the town found itself entrenched in a battle for its very soul. Lucy Rodriguez, a steadfast leader in the quiet rebellion led by the Guardians of Democracy, faced a community at a crossroads. The struggle between the allure of stability and the call of democracy had intensified, leaving the once-harmonious town square a battleground of ideas.

In the aftermath of the community forum, where Lucy had addressed the diverse crowd, the town experienced a brief moment of respite. The echoes of her words lingered in the air, carried by the collective heartbeat of a community grappling with the weight of its choices. The leader, sensing the growing influence of the Guardians of Democracy, responded with a mix of propaganda and increased control.

The town square, once a space for communal gatherings, had transformed into a stage for political theater. Banners celebrating progress fluttered alongside signs expressing dissent, creating a visual tapestry of the town's internal conflict. Police presence remained heightened, casting a shadow over public spaces, and dissenting voices faced subtle forms of intimidation.

Lucy, undeterred by the challenges that lay ahead, continued to organize community forums and outreach initiatives. The bookstore, now a sanctuary for open dialogue, became a hub for residents seeking refuge from the stifling atmosphere outside. The Guardians of Democracy, their numbers swelling with diverse voices, pressed on with their mission to bridge the divides within Millington.

One evening, as Lucy walked through the town square, she encountered Emma Thompson, whose determination remained unyielding despite the challenges they faced.

"Lucy, the leader's influence is growing, but so is our movement. We can't let fear dictate our actions. Millington deserves a future built on openness, not on the suppression of dissent."

Lucy, inspired by Emma's resilience, nodded in agreement. The battle for the soul of Millington was far from over, and the choices made by its residents in the coming days would determine whether the town would succumb to the allure of a curated narrative or rise above the challenges to reclaim the essence of democracy.

The weeks that followed were marked by a dynamic ebb and flow of tension. The leader, recognizing the potency of the Guardians of Democracy's message, escalated efforts to suppress dissent. The police presence in the town square intensified, public gatherings were scrutinized, and dissenting voices faced increased scrutiny.

In response, the Guardians of Democracy expanded their efforts. Small gatherings in neighborhoods became forums for open dialogue, where residents could express their concerns away from the watchful eyes of authority. The movement, fueled by a shared commitment to democratic values, began to permeate every corner of Millington.

One afternoon, as Lucy organized another community forum, she encountered Michael Donovan, whose charismatic presence had been a guiding force in the earlier protests. His eyes reflected a sense of urgency.

"Lucy, the town square is not enough. We need to reach every neighborhood, every corner where the leader's influence has taken root. Our movement must be a reflection of the diversity that defines Millington."

Lucy, recognizing the truth in Michael's words, joined forces with the Guardians of Democracy to expand their outreach. Neighborhood gatherings, town hall meetings in various districts, and small discussions in local businesses became the channels through which the movement sought to rekindle the spirit of open dialogue.

The leader, perhaps sensing the growing resilience of the community, responded with increased efforts to suppress dissent. The town square, once a space for community unity, became a stage for political maneuvering. The police presence intensified, public gatherings were monitored, and those associated with the Guardians of Democracy faced subtle forms of intimidation.

In the face of adversity, Lucy found herself reflecting on the resilience of community. The American nightmare, born out of allegations and chaos, had taken root in Millington, but the spirit of its residents refused to be extinguished. The unraveling threads of democracy, she realized, were not a sign of weakness but a testament to the strength of a community determined to shape its own destiny.

One day, as Lucy walked through the streets, she encountered Mr. Johnson, the war veteran, whose expression conveyed a mixture of concern and determination.

"Lucy, the battle we're facing is not just about the present; it's about the legacy we leave for future generations. We can't allow fear to dictate our choices. The soul of Millington is worth fighting for."

Lucy, inspired by Mr. Johnson's words, nodded in agreement. The town, she realized, stood at a tipping point—a moment where the choices made would define not just the trajectory of Millington but the resilience of democracy itself.

As the weeks unfolded, the struggle within Millington intensified. The leader, seeking to tighten their grip on the narrative, escalated efforts to suppress dissent. The Guardians of Democracy, fueled by a collective determination, expanded their outreach, reaching every neighborhood, every corner where the leader's influence had taken root.

One evening, as Lucy closed the bookstore, she encountered Emma Thompson, whose eyes reflected a mixture of exhaustion and hope.

"Lucy, the town is weary, but we can't give up. The spirit of Millington is alive in every voice that refuses to be silenced. We need to remind everyone that democracy is not a gift but a responsibility we all share."

Lucy, inspired by Emma's resilience, nodded in agreement. The American nightmare, it seemed, had not broken the spirit of Millington but had ignited a flame of determination within its residents. The choices made in the coming days, she realized, would determine not just the fate of the town but the legacy it would leave for generations to come.

The town square, once a symbol of unity, now bore witness to a different kind of conflict. Banners celebrating progress hung alongside signs expressing diverse opinions. The police presence, a silent reminder of authority, coexisted with the growing resilience of a community unwilling to surrender its democratic principles.

One evening, as Lucy stood on the stage in the town square, addressing a diverse crowd that had gathered for a community forum, she felt the weight of responsibility on her shoulders. The American nightmare, born out of allegations and chaos, had taken root in Millington, but the struggle for its soul had become a beacon of hope for communities across the nation.

"Millington," Lucy began, her voice carrying the collective heartbeat of the town, "we stand at a crossroads. The choices we make in the coming days will define the future of our community. Let us not be swayed by fear or the allure of a curated narrative. Instead, let us embrace the diversity of opinions that has long defined us. The soul of Millington is resilient, and together, we can navigate the storm and emerge stronger on the other side."

The crowd, a mosaic of faces reflecting the diversity of Millington, listened with a sense of introspection. The unraveling threads of democracy, Lucy realized, were not a sign of defeat but a call to action—a reminder that the strength of a community lay not in conformity but in the collective courage to question, to resist, and to reclaim the essence of democracy.

As Lucy closed her eyes, bracing herself for the challenges yet to come, she couldn't escape the feeling that the true test of Millington's resilience lay ahead. The town, caught between the allure of stability and the whispers of rebellion, stood at a crossroads where the choices made would echo through the corridors of history. The American nightmare, it seemed, had become a battleground for thevery soul of a community determined to shape its own destiny.

In the quiet moments before the town slept, Lucy couldn't help but reflect on the journey that had brought Millington to this point. The choices made by its residents, she realized, were not just a reflection of the present but a legacy that would endure in the annals of history. The American nightmare, born out of allegations and chaos, had become a catalyst for a movement that transcended the boundaries of one town and resonated with the collective yearning for a future built on the principles that defined a nation.

As Lucy gazed at the stars overhead, she found solace in their silent witness to the struggles and triumphs of a community at the crossroads. The echoes of democracy, she believed, would endure, carried forward by the voices of those who refused to be silenced. The journey, she knew, was far from over, but the resilience of Millington, illuminated by the quiet glow of determination, held the promise of a future where the true spirit of democracy would prevail.

Whispers of Solidarity

In the heart of Millington, where the echoes of democracy met the whispers of rebellion, the town stood at the precipice of a profound transformation. Lucy Rodriguez, a beacon of resilience and determination, found herself at the center of this maelstrom. The struggle for the soul of Millington had become a rallying cry, resonating not only within the town's borders but across the nation.

The town square, once a symbol of unity, now bore witness to a heightened conflict. Banners celebrating progress clashed with signs expressing dissent, creating a visual tapestry that mirrored the internal strife within Millington. The leader's influence, marked by controlled narratives and a carefully curated vision of progress, clashed with the growing resilience of a community unwilling to relinquish its democratic principles.

In the weeks following the pivotal community forum, Millington experienced a surge in tension. The leader, recognizing the influence of the Guardians of Democracy, intensified efforts to suppress dissent. The police presence in the town square became a constant reminder of authority, casting a shadow over public spaces. Dissenting voices faced increased scrutiny, and the battle lines in Millington became more defined.

Undeterred, Lucy and the Guardians of Democracy expanded their efforts.

The bookstore, now a symbol of resistance, continued to serve as a sanctuary for open dialogue. Community forums, neighborhood discussions, and outreach initiatives extended beyond the town square, reaching every corner where the leader's influence had taken root. The movement became a mosaic of voices, reflecting the diversity that defined Millington.

One evening, as Lucy closed the bookstore, she found herself in a quiet conversation with Michael Donovan. The weight of the town's destiny rested on their shoulders, and the resilience of Millington seemed to hinge on the choices made in the coming days.

"Lucy, the town square is a battleground, but our movement is gaining ground in the neighborhoods. We need to amplify the voices of the people, make them heard beyond the propaganda," Michael suggested, his eyes reflecting a blend of determination and concern.

Lucy, appreciating the wisdom in Michael's words, nodded in agreement. The struggle for Millington's soul, she realized, required not just a presence in the town square but a resonance in the hearts and minds of every resident.

In the days that followed, Millington became a town of contrasts. The leader, determined to tighten their grip on the narrative, escalated efforts to suppress dissent. The Guardians of Democracy, fueled by a collective determination, expanded their outreach, conducting town hall meetings, organizing gatherings in local businesses, and fostering open dialogue in every neighborhood.

The bookstore, now a symbol of solidarity, became a nexus for the diverse voices that composed Millington's narrative. Residents, once hesitant to express their dissent, found solace in the embrace of a community that refused to be silenced. Emma Thompson, a stalwart advocate for democracy, became a prominent voice, urging residents to speak their truths.

"Millington, our strength lies not in conformity but in our diversity. Let our voices be a symphony that drowns out the cacophony of propaganda. We stand united, not against our town but for the principles that define us," Emma proclaimed in a passionate speech in the town square.

The response was palpable. The crowd, a tapestry of faces reflecting the myriad backgrounds that defined Millington, resonated with Emma's words. The town square, once a stage for political maneuvering, transformed into a space for communal expression.

However, the leader, feeling the groundswell of dissent, responded with a calculated countermove. The police presence in the town square intensified, and public gatherings faced increased scrutiny. Dissenters, now branded as subversive elements, encountered subtle forms of intimidation. The struggle for Millington's soul had escalated to a level where the consequences of dissent became more pronounced.

In the face of these challenges, Lucy sought to fortify the Guardians of Democracy. The movement, now an amalgamation of diverse voices, faced a critical juncture. The town's resilience, she believed, lay not just in its ability to resist but in its capacity to foster solidarity among its residents.

One day, Lucy received an unexpected visitor at the bookstore—Mr. Johnson, the war veteran whose wisdom had often served as a guiding light in the struggle.

"Lucy, the battleground may be shifting, but the essence of our fight remains the same. Solidarity is our greatest weapon. Let the town square be a testament to our unity," Mr. Johnson advised, his eyes reflecting a blend of experience and hope.

Lucy, inspired by Mr. Johnson's words, took them to heart. The town square, once a contested space, would now become a symbol of collective resistance.

The Guardians of Democracy, along with the residents of Millington, planned a gathering that would transcend the boundaries set by the leader.

As the day of the gathering approached, tension in Millington reached a crescendo. The leader, aware of the impending event, sought to preemptively suppress dissent. The police presence in the town square reached unprecedented levels, and rumors of stricter measures circulated through the community.

Yet, on the chosen day, Millington residents gathered in defiance. The town square, adorned with banners celebrating progress and signs expressing dissent, became a microcosm of the struggle within the town. The Guardians of Democracy, standing alongside Emma Thompson and other vocal advocates, faced the intensified police presence with unwavering determination.

Lucy, standing on the stage in the town square, addressed the gathered crowd with a resonance that echoed through the hearts of the people.

"Millington, our strength lies not just in our resistance but in our unity. The town square, once a contested space, is now a symbol of our collective determination. Let our voices be heard, not as whispers of dissent but as echoes of solidarity. The soul of Millington belongs to its residents, and together, we will reclaim it."

The crowd, a mosaic of determined faces, listened with a shared sense of purpose. The leader's attempt to suppress dissent had inadvertently fueled the flames of Millington's resilience. The town square, once a battleground, had become a stage for the manifestation of unity.

As Lucy closed her eyes, feeling the pulse of the gathering around her, she couldn't help but recognize the significance of the moment. The struggle for Millington's soul had evolved into a movement that transcended the physical boundaries of the town square. The whispers of rebellion, once confined to clandestine conversations, had grown into a resounding declaration of the town's collective identity.

In the aftermath of the gathering, Millington faced a new reality. The leader, shaken by the display of unity, recalibrated their approach. The police presence in the town square, while still notable, became less overt. The bookstore, now a symbol of resilience, continued to serve as a space for open dialogue, and the Guardians of Democracy persisted in their mission to bridge the divides within Millington.

As Millington navigated this precarious equilibrium, Lucy found herself contemplating the journey that had brought the town to this point. The whispers of solidarity, she realized, had not only challenged the leader's narrative but had redefined the narrative of the town itself. The struggle for Millington's soul, born out of the chaos of the American nightmare, had become a beacon of hope for communities across the nation.

In the quiet moments before sleep claimed the town, Lucy Rodriguez, standing on the precipice of history, couldn't escape the feeling that Millington's resilience had become a testament to the enduring spirit of democracy. The echoes of solidarity, she believed, would resonate far beyond the confines of the town, carrying the essence of Millington's struggle to shape its destiny into the corridors of history.

A Tapestry Unraveling

As Millington found itself ensconced in the ebb and flow of dissent and resilience, Lucy Rodriguez, along with the Guardians of Democracy, stood at the forefront of a community teetering on the precipice of transformation. The town square, once a contested space, had become a symbol of unity, but beneath the surface, the fabric of Millington's resilience was still taut, holding the town together in the face of looming challenges.

The weeks that followed the gathering in the town square brought both moments of hope and shadows of uncertainty. The leader, recalibrating their approach in the wake of Millington's display of unity, adopted a more insidious strategy. Propaganda and controlled narratives permeated the airwaves, seeping into the corners of the town where whispers of dissent lingered. The police presence, while less overt in the town square, cast a long shadow over Millington's collective consciousness.

In response, the Guardians of Democracy expanded their efforts to counteract the leader's narrative. Community forums, outreach initiatives, and neighborhood gatherings continued, each serving as a small beacon of resistance against the encroaching darkness. The bookstore, now an emblem of defiance, provided a haven for residents seeking solace from the oppressive atmosphere outside.

One evening, as Lucy closed the bookstore, she encountered Emma Thompson, whose eyes reflected a mixture of determination and weariness.

"Lucy, the town is still caught in a struggle for its soul. The leader may have adjusted their tactics, but we cannot afford to waver. Our movement must persist, for Millington and for the principles we hold dear," Emma proclaimed, her voice resonating with a quiet resolve.

Lucy nodded, acknowledging the truth in Emma's words. The battle for Millington's soul was not won in a single gathering; it was a protracted struggle that required sustained effort and unwavering commitment.

In the days that followed, Millington became a town haunted by the specter of propaganda. The leader's influence, now insidious and pervasive, sought to rewrite the town's narrative. Controlled messages echoed through the airwaves, painting dissenters as subversive elements threatening the stability of the community. The Guardians of Democracy, labeled as agitators, faced increased scrutiny and subtle forms of intimidation.

Undeterred, Lucy and the Guardians of Democracy adapted their strategies. Recognizing the power of storytelling, they launched a grassroots campaign to amplify the voices of Millington's residents. Emma, along with other passionate advocates, shared personal narratives in community forums, emphasizing the shared values that bound the town together.

One afternoon, Lucy organized a storytelling event in the town square, inviting residents to step forward and share their stories. The stage, once a platform for political speeches, transformed into a space for the raw, unfiltered voices of Millington.

A young mother, her voice trembling with emotion, spoke of the dreams she held for her children and the fear that those dreams might be extinguished by the oppressive atmosphere in the town. A war veteran, like Mr. Johnson, shared tales of sacrifice and the belief that the principles for which he fought should not be eroded by the very community he sought to protect.

As the stories unfolded, a tapestry of shared experiences began to weave itself through the crowd. The leader's attempt to control the narrative met a formidable adversary—the authentic voices of Millington's residents.

Yet, even as the community rallied against the encroaching darkness, a sense of unease lingered. The leader, adapting to the changing dynamics, intensified efforts to sow discord among the residents. Whispers of suspicion and mistrust permeated the town, threatening to unravel the fabric of solidarity that had been painstakingly woven.

One evening, Lucy convened an emergency meeting with the Guardians of Democracy. The air in the bookstore, once filled with the optimism of resistance, now carried the weight of concern.

"The leader is employing tactics to divide us from within. We must be vigilant and address the seeds of mistrust before they take root," Lucy asserted, her gaze sweeping across the determined faces of her fellow Guardians.

Michael Donovan, his brow furrowed in contemplation, spoke up, "Lucy's right. Our strength lies in our unity. We cannot allow the leader to exploit our differences. Millington's resilience is built on the diversity of its voices, and we must protect that."

The Guardians of Democracy, recognizing the gravity of the situation, launched an outreach campaign focused on bridging divides. Small group discussions, facilitated by members of the movement, took place in various neighborhoods. Residents shared their concerns, dispelled rumors, and sought common ground amidst the rising tide of mistrust.

In the midst of these efforts, Lucy encountered Mr. Johnson, who had become a revered figure in the struggle for Millington's soul.

"Lucy, the battle is not just against external forces but against the erosion of trust within our community. We must reaffirm our commitment to each other, to the principles that bind us together," Mr. Johnson advised, his voice a steady anchor in the storm.

Inspired by Mr. Johnson's wisdom, Lucy and the Guardians of Democracy organized a town-wide event called "A Night of Unity." The event aimed to bring residents together, fostering open dialogue and rebuilding the sense of community that had sustained Millington through its darkest days.

The night arrived, and the town square, once a symbol of conflict, transformed into a space of shared humanity. Residents, representing the diverse fabric of Millington, engaged in conversations, shared meals, and participated in activities designed to bridge the gaps that had emerged.

Emma, standing on the stage, addressed the gathered crowd, "Millington, we are not defined by the divisions that seek to tear us apart. Our strength lies in our shared humanity, in the bonds that connect us beyond political ideologies. Let this night be a testament to our resilience, to the belief that a united Millington is an unstoppable force."

The response was palpable. As the night unfolded, the tapestry of Millington's unity began to mend. Whispers of solidarity drowned out the lingering whispers of mistrust, and the leader's attempt to divide the community from within faced an unexpected resilience.

However, the night was not without challenges. A small group, influenced by the leader's propaganda, sought to disrupt the event. Tensions flared, and for a moment, it seemed as though the fabric of unity might unravel. In that critical moment, Lucy, Emma, and other vocal advocates stepped forward, diffusing the tension and redirecting the focus to the shared values that bound the community together.

As the night drew to a close, Lucy stood on the stage, surveying the transformed town square. The echoes of unity, she believed, would resonate far beyond this single event. Millington, despite the challenges it faced, had proven its resilience once again. The tapestry, though frayed at the edges, held strong, a testament to the enduring spirit of a community determined to shape its own destiny.

In the quiet aftermath of "A Night of Unity," Lucy found solace in the knowledge that Millington's resilience was not a fleeting illusion but a lived reality. The struggle for the soul of the town continued, but the bonds forged that night would serve as a bulwark against the forces that sought to unravel the fabric of the community.

As Millington settled into the calm after the storm, Lucy couldn't help but feel a glimmer of hope. The whispers of solidarity, once drowned out by the cacophony of propaganda, had emerged stronger. The town, despite the challenges it faced, stood as a testament to the enduring power of unity in the face of adversity. The struggle for Millington's soul, she realized, was an ongoing narrative—a story woven not just by the leader or the Guardians of Democracy but by every resident who refused to let the tapestry unravel.

Echoes of Redemption

In the wake of "A Night of Unity," Millington found itself caught in a delicate equilibrium. The town square, once a battleground of conflicting ideologies, had transformed into a space of shared humanity. Lucy Rodriguez, along with the Guardians of Democracy, navigated the aftermath with a cautious optimism. However, the echoes of redemption resonated against the backdrop of an ongoing struggle for the town's soul.

The leader, recalibrating their approach once again, acknowledged the unexpected resilience of Millington's unity. Propaganda persisted, but the insidious narratives faced a more skeptical audience. The police presence, while still present, adopted a less overt stance. The town, it seemed, had weathered the storm, but the underlying tensions lingered, waiting for the right spark to reignite.

In the days following "A Night of Unity," Lucy and the Guardians of Democracy intensified their efforts to solidify the bonds forged during the event. Small group discussions continued, and community forums expanded to include voices that had previously hesitated to speak out. The bookstore, now a symbol of resilience and open dialogue, flourished as a hub for diverse perspectives.

One evening, as Lucy organized a community forum, she encountered

Michael Donovan, whose eyes reflected a mixture of determination and concern.

"Lucy, the unity we achieved that night was powerful, but we can't underestimate the challenges that still lie ahead. The leader is adapting, and we need to stay ahead of their maneuvers," Michael remarked, his voice a reminder of the ever-evolving nature of the struggle.

Lucy, acknowledging the validity of Michael's concern, replied, "You're right, Michael. Unity is not a one-time achievement; it's an ongoing process. We must remain vigilant and continue to foster open dialogue. Our strength lies in our ability to face challenges together."

In the weeks that followed, Millington experienced a fragile peace. The town square, adorned with remnants of "A Night of Unity," stood as a testament to the collective resilience of its residents. However, beneath the surface, the currents of discontent still flowed. The leader, recognizing the limitations of overt control, sought subtler methods to influence public opinion.

Propaganda campaigns shifted to focus on economic stability and the promise of a secure future. The leader presented themselves as the guardian of Millington's prosperity, weaving a narrative that suggested dissent jeopardized the town's economic well-being. The Guardians of Democracy, labeled as disruptors of stability, faced the challenge of countering this narrative without further deepening the divides within the community.

In response, Lucy and the Guardians devised a strategy to address the economic concerns of residents while reaffirming the importance of democratic values. They organized town hall meetings specifically focused on economic issues, inviting experts to discuss sustainable development and community-driven initiatives. The goal was to demonstrate that unity and economic stability were not mutually exclusive.

One evening, as Lucy prepared for a town hall meeting, she received an unexpected visitor—Emma Thompson, whose resolve remained unyielding.

"Lucy, the leader is exploiting the economic fears of the town. We need to show that democracy is not a threat but a foundation for a prosperous future. Let's use these town hall meetings to reinforce that message," Emma suggested, her eyes reflecting a keen understanding of the delicate balance they sought to achieve.

Lucy agreed, and together they crafted a narrative that emphasized the collaborative potential of Millington's residents. The town hall meetings became a platform for residents to share ideas, propose community projects, and engage in discussions about the kind of future they collectively desired.

As the economic-focused town hall meetings unfolded, Millington witnessed a shift in public discourse. The leader's narrative, centered on the false dichotomy between stability and dissent, faced a growing challenge. Residents began to recognize that a prosperous future could be built on the foundation of open dialogue and shared decision-making.

However, the leader, recognizing the potential erosion of their influence, responded with a more subtle form of manipulation. Community projects proposed during the town hall meetings faced bureaucratic hurdles, and dissenting voices encountered subtle roadblocks. The town, it seemed, was caught in a nuanced struggle where the battleground had shifted from the town square to the administrative corridors.

Undeterred, Lucy and the Guardians of Democracy adapted their strategy once again. They mobilized residents to navigate the bureaucratic challenges collectively, transforming obstacles into opportunities for community solidarity. The bookstore, serving as a coordination hub, became a space for residents to share their experiences and strategize ways to overcome the administrative barriers.

One afternoon, as Lucy facilitated a brainstorming session at the bookstore, she encountered Mr. Johnson, whose quiet wisdom had become a guiding force in the struggle.

"Lucy, bureaucracy is a formidable foe, but the strength of our community lies in our ability to face challenges together. Let's turn these obstacles into a testament of our resilience," Mr. Johnson suggested, his eyes reflecting a lifetime of navigating challenges.

Inspired by Mr. Johnson's words, Lucy and the Guardians launched a campaign called "Bridging Barriers." The campaign aimed to document and address the bureaucratic challenges faced by residents, showcasing their stories in community forums and local media. The goal was to expose the subtle manipulation and present a united front against attempts to stifle the town's democratic spirit.

As the "Bridging Barriers" campaign gained momentum, Millington residents rallied once again. The bookstore, now adorned with stories of resilience, became a living testament to the community's ability to face adversity head-on. The leader, sensing the growing momentum against their manipulative tactics, found themselves on the defensive.

In response, the leader escalated efforts to control the narrative through more aggressive propaganda campaigns. The town square, once a space of unity, became a battleground of conflicting messages. Banners celebrating progress clashed with signs expressing dissent, creating a visual cacophony that mirrored the ideological struggles within the town.

One evening, as Lucy stood on the stage in the town square, addressing a crowd that had gathered for a community forum, she felt the weight of responsibility on her shoulders. The economic challenges, bureaucratic hurdles, and propaganda war had intensified, but the spirit of Millington, she believed, could withstand the storm.

"Millington, the echoes of redemption we felt during 'A Night of Unity' still resonate within us. The struggles we face are not just obstacles but opportunities for us to reaffirm our commitment to each other and to the principles that define our community," Lucy declared, her voice carrying a quiet determination.

The crowd, a tapestry of determined faces reflecting the diverse fabric of Millington, listened with a shared sense of purpose. The economic challenges and bureaucratic hurdles, Lucy realized, were not just individual battles but part of a larger narrative—a story of a town reclaiming its identity in the face of manipulation.

As Lucy closed her eyes, bracing herself for the challenges yet to come, she couldn't escape the feeling that Millington's redemption was not a distant dream but a tangible reality. The struggle for the town's soul, she believed, was a journey of continuous renewal, a narrative woven not just by the leader or the Guardians of Democracy but by every resident who refused to let the echoes of redemption fade away.

Resilience Unveiled

Millington, a town caught in the intricate dance of dissent and unity, found itself at a critical juncture. The struggles that had defined its recent history were not just chapters of a larger narrative but echoes of a resilient spirit yearning to be heard. Lucy Rodriguez, standing on the precipice of the town's destiny, navigated the shifting landscape with a profound sense of responsibility. The town square, once a symbol of conflict, awaited the next chapter of Millington's resilience.

In the aftermath of the intensified propaganda war, Millington stood divided, not just ideologically but emotionally. The leader's manipulative tactics had sown seeds of mistrust, casting a shadow over the unity forged during "A Night of Unity." The town square, adorned with conflicting banners and signs, mirrored the internal strife within the community.

Lucy and the Guardians of Democracy, recognizing the need to address the emotional fractures, initiated a campaign called "Threads of Connection." The campaign aimed to facilitate open and honest conversations among residents, providing a space for people to express their fears, frustrations, and hopes for the future.

One evening, as Lucy prepared for a community forum as part of the "Threads of Connection" campaign, she encountered Emma Thompson, whose resilience remained unshaken.

"Lucy, the emotional fractures run deep, but if we can bridge the gaps in understanding, we can rebuild the bonds that define Millington. Let's use these forums to unravel the threads of connection woven into the fabric of our community," Emma suggested, her eyes reflecting a blend of compassion and determination.

Lucy, inspired by Emma's insight, agreed, "You're right, Emma. The emotional fractures are as significant as the ideological divides. We need to create a space for healing and understanding, where every resident feels seen and heard."

The community forum unfolded in the town square, the stage adorned not with political banners but with symbols of unity and connection. Residents, each carrying the weight of their individual experiences, stepped forward to share their stories. The atmosphere, once tense with ideological conflict, now resonated with a shared vulnerability.

A young couple spoke of their fears for the future and the impact of the town's divisions on their children. An elderly woman shared memories of a time when Millington thrived on community cohesion rather than political discord. The town square, a space once fraught with conflicting ideologies, became a sanctuary for the raw, unfiltered voices of Millington's residents.

As the "Threads of Connection" campaign unfolded, Millington began to witness a subtle transformation. The emotional fractures, laid bare in the town square, became the focal point for collective healing. Small group discussions, facilitated by the Guardians of Democracy, took place in various neighborhoods, providing residents with the opportunity to engage in empathetic conversations.

One day, Lucy encountered Michael Donovan, who had become an advocate for emotional healing within the community.

"Lucy, the stories we're hearing are powerful. They remind us that, beneath the surface, we share common fears, dreams, and struggles. If we can build on these commonalities, we can forge a stronger, more resilient Millington," Michael remarked, his eyes reflecting the emotional depth of the stories they had encountered.

Lucy nodded, acknowledging the significance of the emotional healing process. The town square, once a symbol of conflict, now became a metaphorical weaving loom, where the threads of connection were carefully unraveled and rewoven into a stronger, more resilient fabric.

As Millington embraced the "Threads of Connection" campaign, the emotional fractures began to mend, and a renewed sense of empathy permeated the community. The town square, adorned with symbols of unity, became a space of shared healing rather than ideological conflict.

Yet, the leader, recognizing the potential for this emotional healing to erode their influence, responded with a more insidious strategy. Attempts to sow discord among residents persisted, infiltrating the small group discussions and community forums. The emotional vulnerabilities that had been exposed became targets for manipulation.

In response, Lucy and the Guardians of Democracy intensified their efforts to counteract the leader's divisive tactics. They launched a counter-campaign called "Roots of Resilience," aimed at fortifying the emotional bonds within the community. Through storytelling, art, and communal activities, residents were encouraged to celebrate the shared history and values that defined Millington.

One afternoon, as Lucy prepared for an event as part of the "Roots of Resilience" campaign, she encountered Mr. Johnson, whose quiet wisdom had become a guiding force in the struggle.

"Lucy, emotional resilience is the cornerstone of our community. By celebrating our shared roots, we reinforce the foundations that make us strong. Let's show the leader that Millington's spirit cannot be fractured," Mr. Johnson advised, his eyes reflecting a lifetime of navigating the complexities of human emotions.

Inspired by Mr. Johnson's words, Lucy and the Guardians organized a town-wide celebration called "Harmony Day." The event aimed to showcase the diversity of Millington's residents, not just in terms of ideologies but in the rich tapestry of shared experiences that defined the town.

As Harmony Day unfolded, the town square transformed into a vibrant mosaic of colors, sounds, and emotions. Residents, each carrying a unique story, participated in art installations, storytelling sessions, and communal meals. The emotional resonance of the event echoed through the community, drowning out the leader's attempts to exploit the town's vulnerabilities.

Emma Thompson, standing on the stage, addressed the gathered crowd, "Millington, our resilience lies not just in our ability to weather ideological storms but in our capacity to embrace the emotional tapestry that makes us who we are. Harmony Day is a celebration of our shared roots, our shared struggles, and our shared dreams for the future."

The response was profound. As residents engaged in the festivities, the emotional wounds inflicted by the leader's divisive tactics began to heal. The town square, once a stage for political conflict, became a space of shared joy and connection. The "Threads of Connection" and "Roots of Resilience" campaigns converged, creating a holistic approach to rebuilding Millington's sense of community.

However, the leader, recognizing the potential erosion of their influence, escalated efforts to regain control. Propaganda campaigns intensified, targeting the emotional vulnerabilities exposed during Harmony Day. The town, it seemed, was caught in a relentless struggle where the battleground shifted between ideological conflict and emotional resilience.

In response, Lucy and the Guardians of Democracy adopted a multi-faceted approach. They launched a media campaign to counteract the propaganda, highlighting the genuine connections forged during "Threads of Connection" and the emotional healing experienced on Harmony Day. The town square, once again, became a space for communal resilience, where residents could come together to resist the leader's attempts to sow discord.

As the struggle unfolded, Lucy found herself contemplating the delicate balance between ideological conflict and emotional healing. Millington, she realized, was not just a town defined by its political ideologies but a community bound together by the shared resilience that emerged in the face of adversity.

In the quiet moments before sleep claimed the town, Lucy couldn't escape the feeling that Millington's destiny hung in the balance. The echoes of redemption, woven into the fabric of emotional healing, resonated with a quiet determination. The town square, though still a contested space, held the promise of a future where the threads of connection and roots of resilience would prevail against the divisive forces that sought to unravel the tapestry of Millington's identity.